AWS Elemental MediaStore User Guide

A catalogue record for this book is available from the Hong Kong Public Libraries.

Published in Hong Kong by Samurai Media Limited.

Email: info@samuraimedia.org

ISBN 9789888408047

Contents

What Is AWS Elemental MediaStore?   6

AWS Elemental MediaStore Concepts   7

Related Services   8

Accessing AWS Elemental MediaStore   9

Pricing for AWS Elemental MediaStore   10

Regions for AWS Elemental MediaStore   11

Setting Up AWS Elemental MediaStore   12

Signing Up for AWS   13

Creating an Admin IAM User   14

Creating a Non-Admin IAM User   15

Step 1: Create Policies   16

Step 2: Create User Groups   18

Step 3: Create Users   19

Getting Started with AWS Elemental MediaStore   20
     Step 1: Access AWS Elemental MediaStore 20
     Step 2: Create a Container 20
     Step 3: Upload an Object 20
     Step 4: Access an Object 21

Working with Containers in AWS Elemental MediaStore   22

Rules for Container Names   23

Creating a Container   24

Viewing the Details for a Container   25

Viewing a List of Containers   26

Deleting a Container   27

Working with Container Policies in AWS Elemental MediaStore   28

Viewing a Container Policy   29

Editing a Container Policy   30

Example Container Policies   31

Example Container Policy: Default   32

Example Container Policy: Public Read Access over HTTPS   33

Example Container Policy: Public Read Access over HTTP or HTTPS   34

Example Container Policy: Cross-Account Read Access—HTTP Enabled   35

Example Container Policy: Cross-Account Read Access over HTTPS   36

Example Container Policy: Cross-Account Read Access to a Role   37

Example Container Policy: Cross-Account Full Access to a Role   38

Example Container Policy: Post Access to an AWS Service to a Folder   39

Example Container Policy: Post Access to an AWS Service to Multiple Folders   40

Cross-Origin Resource Sharing (CORS) in AWS Elemental MediaStore   41

CORS Use-case Scenarios   42

Adding a CORS Policy to a Container   43

Viewing a CORS Policy   44

Editing a CORS Policy   45

Deleting a CORS Policy   46

Troubleshooting CORS Issues   47

Example CORS Policies   48

Example CORS Policy: Read Access for Any Domain   49

Example CORS Policy: Read Access for a Specific Domain   50

Working with Folders in AWS Elemental MediaStore   51

Rules for Folder Names   52

Creating a Folder   53

Deleting a Folder   54

Working with Objects in AWS Elemental MediaStore   55

Uploading an Object   56

Viewing a List of Objects   57

Viewing the Details of an Object   59

Downloading an Object   60

Deleting an Object   61

AWS CLI Commands for AWS Elemental MediaStore   62

Monitoring AWS Elemental MediaStore   63

Logging AWS Elemental MediaStore API Calls with AWS CloudTrail   64

AWS Elemental MediaStore Information in CloudTrail   65

Example: AWS Elemental MediaStore Log File Entries   66

Automating AWS Elemental MediaStore with CloudWatch Events   67

AWS Elemental MediaStore Object Upload State-change Event   68

AWS Elemental MediaStore Container State-change Event   69

Working with Content Delivery Networks (CDNs)   70

Allowing Amazon CloudFront to Access Your AWS Elemental MediaStore Container   71

Limits in AWS Elemental MediaStore   72

Document History for User Guide   73

AWS Glossary   74

What Is AWS Elemental MediaStore?

AWS Elemental MediaStore is a video origination and storage service that offers the high performance and immediate consistency required for live origination. With AWS Elemental MediaStore, you can manage video assets as objects in containers to build dependable, cloud-based media workflows.

To use the service, you upload your objects from a source, such as an encoder or data feed, to a container that you create in AWS Elemental MediaStore.

AWS Elemental MediaStore is a great choice for storing fragmented video files when you need strong consistency, low-latency reads and writes, and the ability to handle high volumes of concurrent requests. If you are not delivering live streaming videos, consider using Amazon Simple Storage Service (Amazon S3).

Topics

- AWS Elemental MediaStore Concepts
- Related Services
- Accessing AWS Elemental MediaStore
- Pricing for AWS Elemental MediaStore
- Regions for AWS Elemental MediaStore

AWS Elemental MediaStore Concepts

ARN
An Amazon Resource Name.

Body
The data to be uploaded into an object.

(Byte) range
A subset of object data to be addressed. For more information, see range from the HTTP specification.

Container
A namespace that holds objects. A container has an endpoint that you can use for writing and retrieving objects and attaching access policies.

Endpoint
An entry point to the AWS Elemental MediaStore service, given as an HTTP(S) root URL.

ETag
An entity tag, which is a hash of the object data.

Folder
A division of a container. A folder can hold objects and other folders.

Item
A term used to refer to objects and folders.

Object
An asset, similar to an Amazon S3 object. Objects are the fundamental entities that are stored in AWS Elemental MediaStore. The service accepts all file types.

Origination service
AWS Elemental MediaStore is considered an *origination service* because it is the point of distribution for media content delivery.

Path
A unique identifier for an object or folder, which indicates its location in the container.

Part
A subset of data (chunk) of an object.

Policy
An IAM policy.

AWS Elemental MediaStore verbs Create
Creates an object, often implemented with HTTP POST.

Delete
Deletes an object, often implemented with HTTP DELETE.

Describe
Returns metadata about an object, often implemented with HTTP HEAD.

Get
Retrieves an object.

List
Retrieves a list of items, which can be objects**or folders*.*

Put
Updates an object, often implemented with HTTP PUT.

Related Services

- **Amazon CloudFront** is a global content delivery network (CDN) service that securely delivers data and videos to your viewers. Use CloudFront to deliver content with the best possible performance. For more information, see the Amazon CloudFront Developer Guide.
- **AWS CloudTrail** is a service that lets you monitor the calls made to the CloudTrail API for your account, including calls made by the AWS Management Console, AWS CLI, and other services. For more information, see the AWS CloudTrail User Guide.
- **Amazon CloudWatch** is a monitoring service for AWS cloud resources and the applications that you run on AWS. Use CloudWatch Events to track changes in the status of containers and objects in AWS Elemental MediaStore. For more information, see the Amazon CloudWatch documentation.
- **Amazon S3** is object storage built to store and retrieve any amount of data from anywhere. For more information, see the Amazon S3 documentation.
- **AWS Identity and Access Management (IAM)** is a web service that helps you securely control access to AWS resources for your users. Use IAM to control who can use your AWS resources (authentication) and what resources users can use in which ways (authorization). For more information, see Setting Up AWS Elemental MediaStore.

Accessing AWS Elemental MediaStore

- **AWS Management Console** - The procedures throughout this guide explain how to use the AWS Management Console to perform tasks for AWS Elemental MediaStore.
- **AWS SDKs** – If you're using a programming language that AWS provides an SDK for, you can use an SDK to access AWS Elemental MediaStore. SDKs simplify authentication, integrate easily with your development environment, and provide easy access to AWS Elemental MediaStore commands. For more information, see Tools for Amazon Web Services.
- **AWS Elemental MediaStore API** – If you're using a programming language that an SDK isn't available for, see the AWS Elemental MediaStore API Reference for information about API actions and about how to make API requests.
- **AWS Command Line Interface** – For more information, see the AWS Command Line Interface User Guide.
- **AWS Tools for Windows PowerShell** – For more information, see the AWS Tools for Windows PowerShell User Guide.

Pricing for AWS Elemental MediaStore

As with other AWS products, there are no contracts or minimum commitments for using AWS Elemental MediaStore. You are charged a per GB ingest fee when content enters into the service and a per GB monthly fee for content you store in the service. For more information, see AWS Elemental MediaStore Pricing.

Regions for AWS Elemental MediaStore

To reduce data latency in your applications, AWS Elemental MediaStore offers a regional endpoint to make your requests. To view the list of regions in which AWS Elemental MediaStore is available, see http://docs.aws. amazon.com/general/latest/gr/rande.html#mediastore_region.

Setting Up AWS Elemental MediaStore

Before you start using AWS Elemental MediaStore, you need to sign up for AWS (if you don't already have an AWS account) and create IAM users and roles to allow access to AWS Elemental MediaStore. This includes creating an IAM role for yourself.

Topics

- Signing Up for AWS
- Creating an Admin IAM User
- Creating a Non-Admin IAM User

Signing Up for AWS

If you do not have an AWS account, use the following procedure to create one.

To sign up for AWS

1. Open https://aws.amazon.com/ and choose **Create an AWS Account**.

2. Follow the online instructions.

Creating an Admin IAM User

When you first create an AWS account, you begin with a single sign-in identity that has complete access to all AWS services and resources in the account. This identity is called the AWS account *root user* and is accessed by signing in with the email address and password that you used to create the account. We strongly recommend that you do not use the root user for your everyday tasks, even the administrative ones. Instead, adhere to the best practice of using the root user only to create your first IAM user. Then securely lock away the root user credentials and use them to perform only a few account and service management tasks.

In this procedure, you will use the AWS account root user to create your first IAM user. You will add this IAM user to an Administrators group, to ensure that you have access to all services and their resources in your account. The next time that you access your AWS account, you should sign in with the credentials for this IAM user.

To create an IAM user with limited permissions, see Creating a Non-Admin IAM User.

To create an IAM user for yourself and add the user to an Administrators group

1. Use your AWS account email address and password to sign in as the *AWS account root user* to the IAM console at https://console.aws.amazon.com/iam/. **Note**
   We strongly recommend that you adhere to the best practice of using the **Administrator** IAM user below and securely lock away the root user credentials. Sign in as the root user only to perform a few account and service management tasks.

2. In the navigation pane of the console, choose **Users**, and then choose **Add user**.

3. For **User name**, type **Administrator**.

4. Select the check box next to **AWS Management Console access**, select **Custom password**, and then type the new user's password in the text box. You can optionally select **Require password reset** to force the user to create a new password the next time the user signs in.

5. Choose **Next: Permissions**.

6. On the **Set permissions for user** page, choose **Add user to group**.

7. Choose **Create group**.

8. In the **Create group** dialog box, type **Administrators**.

9. For **Filter**, choose **Job function**.

10. In the policy list, select the check box for **AdministratorAccess**. Then choose **Create group**.

11. Back in the list of groups, select the check box for your new group. Choose **Refresh** if necessary to see the group in the list.

12. Choose **Next: Review** to see the list of group memberships to be added to the new user. When you are ready to proceed, choose **Create user**.

You can use this same process to create more groups and users, and to give your users access to your AWS account resources. To learn about using policies to restrict users' permissions to specific AWS resources, go to Access Management and Example Policies.

Creating a Non-Admin IAM User

Users in the Administrators group for an account have access to all AWS services and resources in that account. This section describes how to create users with permissions that are limited to AWS Elemental MediaStore.

Topics

- Step 1: Create Policies
- Step 2: Create User Groups
- Step 3: Create Users

Step 1: Create Policies

Create two policies for AWS Elemental MediaStore: one to provide read/write access and one to provide read-only access. Perform these steps one time only for each policy.

To create policies

1. Use your AWS account ID or account alias, and the credentials for your admin IAM user to sign in to the IAM console.

2. In the navigation pane of the console, choose **Policies**, and then choose **Create policy**.

3. Choose the **JSON** tab and paste the following policy:

```
1  {
2      "Version": "2012-10-17",
3      "Statement": [
4          {
5              "Action": [
6                  "mediastore:*"
7              ],
8              "Effect": "Allow",
9              "Resource": "*",
10             "Condition": {
11                 "Bool": {
12                     "aws:SecureTransport": "true"
13                 }
14             }
15         }
16     ]
17 }
```

This policy allows all actions on all resources in AWS Elemental MediaStore.

4. Choose **Review policy**.

5. On the **Review policy** page, for **Name**, type **MediaStoreAllAccess** , and then choose **Create policy**.

6. On the **Policies** page, repeat steps 1-5 to create a read-only policy. Use the following policy and call it **MediaStoreReadOnlyAccess**:

```
1  {
2      "Version": "2012-10-17",
3      "Statement": [
4          {
5              "Action": [
6                  "mediastore:Get*",
7
8                  "mediastore:List*",
9                  "mediastore:Describe*"
10             ],
11             "Effect": "Allow",
12             "Resource": "*",
13             "Condition": {
14                 "Bool": {
15                     "aws:SecureTransport": "true"
16                 }
17             }
```

```
18          }
19      ]
20  }
```

Step 2: Create User Groups

You can create a user group for each policy and assign users to a group rather than attaching individual policies to each user. Using the steps below, create two user groups: one for the **MediaStoreAllAccess** policy and one for the **MediaStoreReadOnlyAccess** policy.

To create user groups

1. In the navigation pane of the IAM console, choose **Groups**, and then choose **Create New Group**.

2. On the **Set Group Name** page, type a name for the group, such as **MediaStoreAdmins**.

3. Choose **Next Step**.

4. On the **Attach Policy** page, for **Filter**, choose **Customer Managed**.

5. In the policy list, choose the **MediaStoreAllAccess** policy that you created.

6. Choose **Next Step**.

7. On the **Review** page, verify that the correct policies are added to this group, and then choose **Create Group**.

8. On the **Groups** page, repeat steps 1-7 to create a user group with a read-only permissions. Use the following guidelines:

   - In step 2, type a group name such as **MediaStoreReaders**.
   - In step 4, choose the **MediaStoreReadOnlyAccess** policy.

Step 3: Create Users

Create IAM users for the individuals who require access to AWS Elemental MediaStore, and add each user to the appropriate user group to ensure that they have the right level of permissions. If you already have users created, skip to step 6 to modify the permissions for the users.

To create users

1. In the navigation pane of the IAM console, choose **Users**, and then choose **Add user**.

2. For **User name**, type the name that the user will use to sign in to AWS Elemental MediaStore.

3. Select the check box next to **AWS Management Console access**, select **Custom password**, and then type the new user's password in the box. You can optionally select **Require password reset** to force the user to create a password the next time the user signs in.

4. Choose **Next: Permissions**.

5. On the **Set permissions for user** page, choose **Add user to group**.

6. In the group list, choose the group with the appropriate attached policy. Remember that permissions levels are as follows:

   - The **MediaStoreAdmins** group has permissions that allow all actions on all resources in AWS Elemental MediaStore.
   - The **MediaStoreReaders** group has permissions that allow read-only rights for all resources in AWS Elemental MediaStore.

7. Choose **Next: Review** to see the list of group memberships to be added to the new user.

8. When you are ready to proceed, choose **Create user**.

Getting Started with AWS Elemental MediaStore

This Getting Started tutorial shows you how to use AWS Elemental MediaStore to create a container and upload an object.

Topics

- Step 1: Access AWS Elemental MediaStore
- Step 2: Create a Container
- Step 3: Upload an Object
- Step 4: Access an Object

Step 1: Access AWS Elemental MediaStore

Once you have set up your AWS account and created IAM users and roles, you sign in to the console for AWS Elemental MediaStore.

To access AWS Elemental MediaStore

- Sign in to the AWS Management Console and open the AWS Elemental MediaStore console at https://console.aws.amazon.com/mediastore/. **Note**
  You can login using any of the IAM credentials you have created for this account. For information about creating IAM credentials, see Setting Up AWS Elemental MediaStore.

Step 2: Create a Container

You use containers in AWS Elemental MediaStore to store your folders and objects. You can use containers to group related objects in the same way that you use a directory to group files in a file system. You aren't charged when you create containers; you are charged only when you upload an object to a container.

To create a container

1. On the **Containers** page, choose **Create container**.

2. For **Container name**, type a name for your container. For more information, see Rules for Container Names.

3. Choose **Create container**. AWS Elemental MediaStore adds the new container to a list of containers. Initially, the status of the container is **Creating**, and then it changes to **Active**.

Step 3: Upload an Object

You can upload objects (up to 10 MB each) to a container or to a folder within a container. To upload an object to a folder, you specify the path to the folder. If the folder already exists, AWS Elemental MediaStore stores the object in the folder. If the folder doesn't exist, the service creates it, and then stores the object in the folder.

Note
Object file names can contain only letters, numbers, periods (.), underscores (_), tildes (~), and hyphens (-).

To upload an object

1. On the **Containers** page, choose the name of the container that you just created. The details page for the container appears.

2. Choose **Upload object**.

3. For **Target path**, type a path for the folders. For example, `premium/canada`. If any of the folders in the path don't exist yet, AWS Elemental MediaStore creates them automatically.

4. For **Object**, choose **Browse**.

5. Navigate to the appropriate folder, and choose one object to upload.

6. Choose **Open**, and then choose **Upload**.

Step 4: Access an Object

You can download your objects to a specified endpoint.

1. On the **Containers** page, choose the name of the container that has the object that you want to download.

2. If the object that you want to download is in a subfolder, continue choosing the folder names until you see the object.

3. Choose the name of the object.

4. On the details page for the object, choose **Download**.

Working with Containers in AWS Elemental MediaStore

You use containers in AWS Elemental MediaStore to store your folders and objects. Related objects can be grouped in containers in the same way that you use a directory to group files in a file system. You aren't charged when you create containers; you are charged only when you upload an object to a container. For more information about charges, see AWS Elemental MediaStore Pricing.

Topics

- Rules for Container Names
- Creating a Container
- Viewing the Details for a Container
- Viewing a List of Containers
- Deleting a Container

Rules for Container Names

Container names must follow these rules:

- Must be unique across all existing container names in AWS Elemental MediaStore. One way to help ensure uniqueness is to prefix your container names with the name of your organization.
- Is case sensitive. For example, you can have a container named `myContainer` and a folder named `mycontainer` because those names are unique.
- Can't be renamed after it has been created.
- Can contain uppercase letters, lowercase letters, numbers, and underscores (_).
- Must be from 3 to 255 characters long.

Creating a Container

You can create up to 100 containers for each AWS account. However, there is no limit to the number of folders that you can create in each of those containers. In addition, there is no limit to the number of objects that you can upload to each container.

To create a container (console)

1. Open the AWS Elemental MediaStore console at https://console.aws.amazon.com/mediastore/.

2. On the **Containers** page, choose **Create container**.

3. For **Container** name, type a name for the container. For more information, see Rules for Container Names.

4. Choose **Create container**. AWS Elemental MediaStore adds the new container to a list of containers. Initially, the status of the container is **Creating**, and then it changes to **Active**.

To create a container (AWS CLI)

- In the AWS CLI, use the **create-container** command.

  Example:

```
1 aws mediastore --region us-west-2 create-container --container-name=ExampleContainer
```

  Example return value:

```
1 {
2     "Container": {
3         "Status": "CREATING",
4         "CreationTime": 1506528818.0,
5         "Name": "ExampleContainer",
6         "ARN": "arn:aws:mediastore:us-west-2:111222333444:container/ExampleContainer"
7     }
8 }
```

Viewing the Details for a Container

Details for a container include the container policy, endpoint, ARN, and creation time.

To view the details for a container (console)

1. Open the AWS Elemental MediaStore console at https://console.aws.amazon.com/mediastore/.

2. On the **Containers** page, choose the name of the container.

   The container details page appears. This page is divided into two sections:

   - The **Objects** section, which lists the objects and folders in the container.
   - The **Container** policy section, which shows the resource-based policy that is associated with this container. For information about resource policies, see .

To view the details for a container (AWS CLI)

- In the AWS CLI, use the **describe-container** command.

  Example:

```
1 aws mediastore --region us-west-2 describe-container --container-name=ExampleContainer
```

  Example return value:

```
1 {
2     "Container": {
3         "Status": "ACTIVE",
4         "Endpoint": "https://aaabbbcccdddee.data.mediastore.us-west-2.amazonaws.com",
5         "CreationTime": 1506528818.0,
6         "Name": "ExampleContainer",
7         "ARN": "arn:aws:mediastore:us-west-2:111222333444:container/ExampleContainer"
8     }
9 }
```

Viewing a List of Containers

You can view a list of all the containers that are associated with your account.

To view a list of containers (console)

- Open the AWS Elemental MediaStore console at https://console.aws.amazon.com/mediastore/.

  The **Containers** page appears, listing all the containers that are associated with your account.

To view a list of containers (AWS CLI)

- In the AWS CLI, use the **list-containers** command.

  Example:

```
1 aws mediastore --region us-west-2 list-containers
```

  Example return value:

```
1  {
2      "Inputs": [
3          {
4      "Containers": [
5          {
6              "Status": "ACTIVE",
7              "Endpoint": "https://aaabbbcccdddee.data.mediastore.us-west-2.amazonaws.com",
8              "CreationTime": 1505317931.0,
9              "Name": "ExampleLiveDemo",
10             "ARN": "arn:aws:mediastore:us-west-2:111222333444:container/ExampleLiveDemo"
11         },
12         {
13             "Status": "ACTIVE",
14             "Endpoint": "https://fffggghhhiiijj.data.mediastore.us-west-2.amazonaws.com",
15             "CreationTime": 1506528818.0,
16             "Name": "ExampleContainer",
17             "ARN": "arn:aws:mediastore:us-west-2:111222333444:container/ExampleContainer"
18         }
19     ]
20 }
```

Deleting a Container

You can delete a container only if it has no objects.

To delete a container (console)

1. Open the AWS Elemental MediaStore console at https://console.aws.amazon.com/mediastore/.

2. On the **Containers** page, choose the radio button to the left of the container name.

3. Choose **Delete**.

To delete a container (AWS CLI)

- In the AWS CLI, use the **delete-container** command.

  Example:

  ```
  1 aws mediastore --region us-west-2 delete-container --container-name=ExampleLiveDemo
  ```

  This command has no return value.

Working with Container Policies in AWS Elemental MediaStore

Each container has a resource-based policy that governs access rights to all folders and objects in that container. The default policy, which is automatically attached to all new containers, allows access to all AWS Elemental MediaStore operations on the container. It specifies that this access has the condition of requiring HTTPS for the operations. Once you have created a container, you can edit the policy assigned to that container.

Topics

- Viewing a Container Policy
- Editing a Container Policy
- Example Container Policies

Viewing a Container Policy

You can use the console or the AWS CLI to view the resource-based policy of a container.

To view a container policy (console)

1. Open the AWS Elemental MediaStore console at https://console.aws.amazon.com/mediastore/.

2. On the **Containers** page, choose the container name.

   The container details page appears. The policy is displayed in the **Container policy** section.

To view a container policy (AWS CLI)

- In the AWS CLI, use the **get-container-policy** command.

  Example:

```
1 aws mediastore get-container-policy --container-name=ExampleLiveDemo --region us-west-2
```

  Example return value

```
1  {
2    "Policy": {
3      "Version": "2012-10-17",
4      "Statement": [
5        {
6          "Sid": "MediaStoreFullAccess",
7          "Effect": "Allow",
8          "Principal": "*",
9          "Action": "mediastore:*",
10         "Resource": "arn:aws:mediastore:us-west-2:111222333444:container/ExampleLiveDemo
               /*",
11         "Condition": {
12           "Bool": {
13             "aws:SecureTransport": "true"
14           }
15         }
16       }
17     ]
18   }
19 }
```

Editing a Container Policy

You can edit the permissions in the default container policy, or you can create a new policy that replaces the default policy. It takes 5 minutes for the new policy to become effective.

To edit a container policy (console)

1. Open the AWS Elemental MediaStore console at https://console.aws.amazon.com/mediastore/.

2. On the **Containers** page, choose the container name.

3. Choose **Edit policy**. For examples that show how to set different permissions, see Example Container PoliciesExample CORS Policies.

4. Make the appropriate changes, and then choose **Save**.

To edit a container policy (AWS CLI)

- In the AWS CLI, use the **put-container-policy** command.

  Example:

```
1 aws mediastore put-container-policy --region us-west-2 --container-name ExampleLiveDemo --
      policy-name=default --policy={\"Version\" : \"2012-10-17\",  \"Statement\" : [ {    \"
      Sid\" : \"MediaStoreFullAccess\",    \"Effect\" : \"Allow\",    \"Principal\" : \"*\",
        \"Action\" : \"mediastore:*\",    \"Resource\" : \"arn:aws:mediastore:us-west
      -2:111222333444:container/ExampleLiveDemo/*\",    \"Condition\" : {      \"Bool\" : {
          \"aws:SecureTransport\" : \"true\"        }    }  } ]}"
2 }
```

  This command has no return value.

Example Container Policies

The following examples show container policies constructed for different user groups.

Topics

- Example Container Policy: Default
- Example Container Policy: Public Read Access over HTTPS
- Example Container Policy: Public Read Access over HTTP or HTTPS
- Example Container Policy: Cross-Account Read Access—HTTP Enabled
- Example Container Policy: Cross-Account Read Access over HTTPS
- Example Container Policy: Cross-Account Read Access to a Role
- Example Container Policy: Cross-Account Full Access to a Role
- Example Container Policy: Post Access to an AWS Service to a Folder
- Example Container Policy: Post Access to an AWS Service to Multiple Folders

Example Container Policy: Default

When you create a container, AWS Elemental MediaStore automatically attaches the following resource-based policy:

```
1  {
2    "Version": "2012-10-17",
3    "Statement": [
4      {
5        "Sid": "MediaStoreFullAccess",
6        "Action": [ "mediastore:*" ],
7        "Principal":{
8          "AWS" : "arn:aws:iam::<aws_account_number>:root"},
9        "Effect": "Allow",
10       "Resource": "arn:aws:mediastore:<region>:<owner acct number>:container/<container name
            >/*",
11       "Condition": {
12         "Bool": { "aws:SecureTransport": "true" }
13       }
14     }
15   ]
16 }
```

The policy is built into the service, so you don't have to create it. The default policy can't be changed; however, you can edit a container's policy.

The default policy that is assigned to all new containers allows access to all AWS Elemental MediaStore operations on the container. It specifies that this access has the condition of requiring HTTPS for the operations.

Example Container Policy: Public Read Access over HTTPS

This policy allows users to retrieve an object through an HTTPS request. It allows this access to all users who are authenticated. The statement has the name `PublicReadOverHttps`. It allows access to the `GetObject` and `DescribeObject` operations on any object (as specified by the * at the end of the resource path). It allows this access to absolutely anyone: all authenticated users and anonymous users (users who are not logged in). It specifies that this access has the condition of requiring HTTPS for the operations:

```
 1  {
 2    "Version": "2012-10-17",
 3    "Statement": [
 4      {
 5        "Sid": "PublicReadOverHttps",
 6        "Effect": "Allow",
 7        "Action": ["mediastore:GetObject", "mediastore:DescribeObject"],
 8        "Principal": "*",
 9        "Resource": "arn:aws:mediastore:<region>:<owner acct number>:container/<container name
              >/*",
10        "Condition": {
11          "Bool": {
12              "aws:SecureTransport": "true"
13          }
14        }
15      }
16    ]
17  }
```

Example Container Policy: Public Read Access over HTTP or HTTPS

This policy allows access to the `GetObject` and `DescribeObject` operations on any object (as specified by the * at the end of the resource path). It allows this access to anyone, including all authenticated users and anonymous users (users who are not logged in):

```
1  {
2    "Version": "2012-10-17",
3    "Statement": [
4      {
5        "Sid": "PublicReadOverHttpOrHttps",
6        "Effect": "Allow",
7        "Action": ["mediastore:GetObject", "mediastore:DescribeObject"],
8        "Principal": "*",
9        "Resource": "arn:aws:mediastore:<region>:<owner acct number>:container/<container name
            >/*",
10       "Condition": {
11         "Bool": { "aws:SecureTransport": ["true", "false"] }
12       }
13     }
14   ]
15 }
```

Example Container Policy: Cross-Account Read Access—HTTP Enabled

This policy allows users to retrieve an object through an HTTP request. It allows this access to authenticated users with cross-account access. The object is not required to be hosted on a server with an SSL certificate:

```
1  {
2    "Version" : "2012-10-17",
3    "Statement" : [ {
4      "Sid" : "CrossAccountReadOverHttpOrHttps",
5      "Effect" : "Allow",
6      "Principal" : {
7        "AWS" : "arn:aws:iam::<other acct number>:root"
8      },
9      "Action" : [ "mediastore:GetObject", "mediastore:DescribeObject" ],
10     "Resource" : "arn:aws:mediastore:<region>:<owner acct number>:container/<container name>/*",
11     "Condition" : {
12       "Bool" : {
13         "aws:SecureTransport" : [ "true", "false" ]
14       }
15     }
16   } ]
17 }
```

Example Container Policy: Cross-Account Read Access over HTTPS

This policy allows access to the `GetObject` and `DescribeObject` operations on any object (as specified by the * at the end of the resource path) that is owned by root user user of the specified . It specifies that this access has the condition of requiring HTTPS for the operations:

```
1  {
2    "Version": "2012-10-17",
3    "Statement": [
4      {
5        "Sid": "CrossAccountReadOverHttps",
6        "Effect": "Allow",
7        "Action": ["mediastore:GetObject", "mediastore:DescribeObject"],
8        "Principal":{
9          "AWS": "arn:aws:iam::<other acct number>:root"},
10       "Resource": "arn:aws:mediastore:<region>:<owner acct number>:container/<container name
              >/*",
11       "Condition": {
12         "Bool": {
13             "aws:SecureTransport": "true"
14         }
15       }
16     }
17   ]
18 }
```

Example Container Policy: Cross-Account Read Access to a Role

The policy allows access to the `GetObject` and `DescribeObject` operations on any object (as specified by the *
at the end of the resource path) that is owned by the . It allows this access to any user of the if that account has
assumed the role that is specified in :

```
1  {
2    "Version": "2012-10-17",
3    "Statement": [
4      {
5        "Sid": "CrossAccountRoleRead",
6        "Effect": "Allow",
7        "Action": ["mediastore:GetObject", "mediastore:DescribeObject"],
8        "Principal":{
9          "AWS": "arn:aws:iam::<other acct number>:role/<role name>"},
10       "Resource": "arn:aws:mediastore:<region>:<owner acct number>:container/<container name
             >/*",
11     }
12   ]
13 }
```

Example Container Policy: Cross-Account Full Access to a Role

This policy allows users with cross-account access to update any object in the account, as long as the user is logged in over HTTP. It also allows users with cross-account access to delete, download, and describe objects over HTTP or HTTPS:

- The first statement is `CrossAccountRolePostOverHttps`. It allows access to the `PutObject` operation on any object and allows this access to any user of the specified account if that account has assumed the role that is specified in . It specifies that this access has the condition of requiring HTTPS for the operation (this condition must always be included when providing access to `PutObject`).

  In other words, any principal that has cross-account access can access `PutObject`, but only over HTTPS.

- The second statement is `CrossAccountFullAccessExceptPost`. It allows access to all operations except `PutObject` on any object. It allows this access to any user of the specified account if that account has assumed the role that is specified in . This access does not have the condition of requiring HTTPS for the operations.

  In other words, any account that has cross-account access can access `DeleteObject`, `GetObject`, and so on (but not `PutObject`), and can do this over HTTP or HTTPS.

  If you don't exclude `PutObject` from the second statement, the statement won't be valid (because if you include `PutObject` you must explicitly set HTTPS as a condition).

```
1  {
2    "Version": "2012-10-17",
3    "Statement": [
4      {
5        "Sid": "CrossAccountRolePostOverHttps",
6        "Effect": "Allow",
7        "Action": "mediastore:PutObject",
8        "Principal":{
9          "AWS": "arn:aws:iam::<other acct number>:role/<role name>"},
10       "Resource": "arn:aws:mediastore:<region>:<owner acct number>:container/<container name
            >/*",
11       "Condition": {
12         "Bool": {
13            "aws:SecureTransport": "true"
14         }
15       }
16     },
17     {
18       "Sid": "CrossAccountFullAccessExceptPost",
19       "Effect": "Allow",
20       "NotAction": "mediastore:PutObject",
21       "Principal":{
22         "AWS": "arn:aws:iam::<other acct number>:role/<role name>"},
23       "Resource": "arn:aws:mediastore:<region>:<owner acct number>:container/<container name>/*"
24     }
25   ]
26 }
```

Example Container Policy: Post Access to an AWS Service to a Folder

This policy allows another AWS service to post objects in AWS Elemental MediaStore. It allows access to `PutObject` on any object and allows this access to a specific AWS service. It specifies that this access has the condition of requiring HTTPS for the operation (this condition must always be included when providing access to `PutObject`).

```
1  {
2    "Version": "2012-10-17",
3    "Statement": [
4      {
5        "Sid": "MediaStorePostToSpecificPath",
6        "Effect": "Allow",
7        "Action": "mediastore:PutObject",
8        "Principal":{
9          "AWS": "<aws service principal>"},
10       "Resource": "arn:aws:mediastore:<region>:<owner acct number>:container/<container name>/<
             specific path>/*",
11       "Condition": {
12       "Bool": {
13           "aws:SecureTransport": "true"
14       }
15     }
16   }
17  ]
18 }
```

Example Container Policy: Post Access to an AWS Service to Multiple Folders

This policy is a variation on `MediaStorePostToSpecificPath` that shows how to set up access to two different paths:

```
1  {
2    "Version": "2012-10-17",
3    "Statement": [
4      {
5        "Sid": "MediaStorePostToSeveralPaths",
6        "Effect": "Allow",
7        "Action": "mediastore:PutObject",
8        "Principal":{
9          "AWS": "<aws service principal>"},
10       "Resource": [
11         "arn:aws:mediastore:<region>:<owner acct number>:container/<container name>/<specific
                path 1>/*",
12         "arn:aws:mediastore:<region>:<owner acct number>:container/<container name>/<specific
                path 2>/*",
13       ],
14       "Condition": {
15         "Bool": {
16             "aws:SecureTransport": "true"
17         }
18       }
19     }
20   ]
21 }
```

Cross-Origin Resource Sharing (CORS) in AWS Elemental MediaStore

Cross-origin resource sharing (CORS) defines a way for client web applications that are loaded in one domain to interact with resources in a different domain. With CORS support in AWS Elemental MediaStore, you can build rich client-side web applications with AWS Elemental MediaStore and selectively allow cross-origin access to your AWS Elemental MediaStore resources.

This section provides an overview of CORS. The subtopics describe how you can enable CORS using the AWS Elemental MediaStore console, or programmatically using the AWS Elemental MediaStore REST API and the AWS SDKs.

Topics

- CORS Use-case Scenarios
- Adding a CORS Policy to a Container
- Viewing a CORS Policy
- Editing a CORS Policy
- Deleting a CORS Policy
- Troubleshooting CORS Issues
- Example CORS Policies

CORS Use-case Scenarios

The following are example scenarios for using CORS:

- Scenario 1: Suppose you are distributing live streaming video in an AWS Elemental MediaStore container named *LiveVideo*. Your users load the video manifest endpoint `http://livevideo.mediastore.ap-southeast-2.amazonaws.com` from a specific origin like `www.example.com`. You want to use a JavaScript video player to access videos that are originated from this container via unauthenticated `GET` and `PUT` requests. A browser would typically block JavaScript from allowing those requests, but you can set a CORS policy on your container to explicitly enable these requests from `www.example.com`.
- Scenario 2: Suppose you want to host the same live stream as in Scenario 1 from your AWS Elemental MediaStore container, but want to allow requests from any origin. You can configure a CORS policy to allow wildcard (*) origins, so that requests from any origin can access the video.

Adding a CORS Policy to a Container

This section explains how to add a cross-origin resource sharing (CORS) configuration to an AWS Elemental MediaStore container. CORS allows client web applications that are loaded in one domain to interact with resources in another domain.

To configure your container to allow cross-origin requests, you add a CORS policy to the container. A CORS policy defines rules that identify the origins that you allow to access your container, the operations (HTTP methods) supported for each origin, and other operation-specific information.

When you add a CORS policy to the container, the container policies (that govern access rights to the container) continue to apply.

To add a CORS policy (console)

1. Open the AWS Elemental MediaStore console at https://console.aws.amazon.com/mediastore/.

2. On the **Containers** page, choose the name of the container that you want to create a CORS policy for.

   The container details page appears.

3. In the **Container CORS policy** section, choose **Create CORS policy**.

4. Insert the policy in JSON format, and then choose **Save**.

To add a CORS policy (AWS CLI)

- In the AWS CLI, use the `put-cors-policy` command.

  Example:

```
1 aws mediastore put-cors-policy --container-name ExampleContainer --cors-policy '[{"
    AllowedOrigins": ["*"],"AllowedMethods": ["GET"],"AllowedHeaders": ["*"],"ExposeHeaders
    ": ["*"], "MaxAgeSeconds":3000}]' --region ap-southeast-2 --endpoint https://mediastore
    .ap-southeast-2.amazonaws.com/
```

  This command has no return value.

Viewing a CORS Policy

Cross-origin resource sharing (CORS) defines a way for client web applications that are loaded in one domain to interact with resources in a different domain.

To view a CORS policy (console)

1. Open the AWS Elemental MediaStore console at https://console.aws.amazon.com/mediastore/.

2. On the **Containers** page, choose the name of the container that you want to view the CORS policy for.

   The container details page appears, with the CORS policy in the **Container CORS policy** section.

To view a CORS policy (AWS CLI)

- In the AWS CLI, use the `get-cors-policy` command.

  Example:

```
1 aws mediastore get-cors-policy --container-name ExampleContainer --region ap-southeast-2 --
      endpoint https://mediastore.ap-southeast-2.amazonaws.com/
```

  Example return value:

```
1  [
2    {
3      "AllowedOrigins": ["http://example.com"],
4      "AllowedMethods": ["GET"],
5      "AllowedHeaders": ["*"],
6      "MaxAgeSeconds": 3000
7    },
8    {
9      "AllowedOrigins": ["https://*"],
10     "AllowedMethods": ["GET", "PUT"],
11     "AllowedHeaders": ["x-amzn*"],
12     "MaxAgeSeconds": 0
13   }
14 ]
```

Editing a CORS Policy

Cross-origin resource sharing (CORS) defines a way for client web applications that are loaded in one domain to interact with resources in a different domain.

To edit a CORS policy (console)

1. Open the AWS Elemental MediaStore console at https://console.aws.amazon.com/mediastore/.

2. On the **Containers** page, choose the name of the container that you want to edit the CORS policy for.

   The container details page appears.

3. In the **Container CORS policy** section, choose **Edit CORS policy**.

4. Make your changes to the policy, and then choose **Save**.

Deleting a CORS Policy

Cross-origin resource sharing (CORS) defines a way for client web applications that are loaded in one domain to interact with resources in a different domain. Deleting the CORS policy from a container removes permissions for cross-origin requests.

To delete a CORS policy (console)

1. Open the AWS Elemental MediaStore console at https://console.aws.amazon.com/mediastore/.

2. On the **Containers** page, choose the name of the container that you want to delete the CORS policy for.

   The container details page appears.

3. In the **Container CORS policy** section, choose **Edit CORS policy**.

4. Clear the text from the text box, and then choose **Save**.

To delete a CORS policy (AWS CLI)

- In the AWS CLI, use the `delete-cors-policy` command.

  Example:

```
1 aws mediastore delete-cors-policy --container-name ExampleContainer --region ap-southeast-2
    --endpoint https://mediastore.ap-southeast-2.amazonaws.com/
```

  This command has no return value.

Troubleshooting CORS Issues

If you encounter unexpected behavior when you access a container that has a CORS policy, follow these steps to troubleshoot the issue.

1. Verify that the CORS policy is attached to the container.

   For instructions, see Viewing a CORS Policy.

2. Capture the complete request and response using a tool of your choice (such as your browser's developer console). Verify that the CORS policy that is attached to the container includes at least one CORS rule that matches the data in your request, as follows:

   1. Verify that the request has an `Origin` header.

      If the header is missing, AWS Elemental MediaStore does not treat the request as a cross-origin request and does not send CORS response headers back in the response.

   2. Verify that the `Origin` header in your request matches at least one of the `AllowedOrigins` elements in the specific `CORSRule`.

      The scheme, the host, and the port values in the `Origin` request header must match the `AllowedOrigins` in the `CORSRule`. For example, if you set `CORSRule` to allow the origin `http://www.example.com`, then both `https://www.example.com` and `http://www.example.com:80` origins in your request do not match the allowed origin in your configuration.

   3. Verify that the method in your request (or the method specified in the `Access-Control-Request-Method` in case of a preflight request) is one of the `AllowedMethods` elements in the same `CORSRule`.

   4. For a preflight request, if the request includes an `Access-Control-Request-Headers` header, verify that the `CORSRule` includes the `AllowedHeaders` entries for each value in the `Access-Control-Request-Headers` header.

Example CORS Policies

The following examples show cross-origin resource sharing (CORS) policies.

Topics

- Example CORS Policy: Read Access for Any Domain
- Example CORS Policy: Read Access for a Specific Domain

Example CORS Policy: Read Access for Any Domain

The following policy allows a webpage from any domain to retrieve content from your AWS Elemental MediaStore container. The request includes all HTTP headers from the originating domain, and the service responds only to HTTP GET and HTTP HEAD requests from the originating domain. The results are cached for 3,000 seconds before a new set of results is delivered.

```
1  [
2    {
3      "AllowedHeaders": [
4        "*"
5      ],
6      "AllowedMethods": [
7        "GET",
8        "HEAD"
9      ],
10     "AllowedOrigins": [
11       "*"
12     ],
13     "MaxAgeSeconds": 3000
14   }
15 ]
```

Example CORS Policy: Read Access for a Specific Domain

The following policy allows a webpage from `https://www.example.com` to retrieve content from your AWS Elemental MediaStore container. The request includes all HTTP headers from `https://www.example.com`, and the service responds only to HTTP GET and HTTP HEAD requests from `https://www.example.com`. The results are cached for 3,000 seconds before a new set of results is delivered.

```
1  [
2    {
3      "AllowedHeaders": [
4        "*"
5      ],
6      "AllowedMethods": [
7        "GET",
8        "HEAD"
9      ],
10     "AllowedOrigins": [
11       "https://www.example.com"
12     ],
13     "MaxAgeSeconds": 3000
14   }
15 ]
```

Working with Folders in AWS Elemental MediaStore

Folders are divisions within a container. You use folders to subdivide your container in the same way that you create subfolders to divide a folder in a file system. You can create up to 10 levels of folders (not including the container itself).

Folders are optional; you can choose to upload your objects directly to a container instead of a folder. However, folders are an easy way to organize your objects.

To upload an object to a folder, you specify the path to the folder. If the folder already exists, AWS Elemental MediaStore stores the object in the folder. If the folder doesn't exist, the service creates it, and then stores the object in the folder.

For example, suppose you have a container named `movies`, and you upload a file named `mlaw.ts` with the path `premium/canada`. AWS Elemental MediaStore stores the object in the subfolder canada under the folder premium. If neither folder exists, the service creates both the `premium` folder and the `canada` subfolder, and then stores your object in the `canada` subfolder. If you specify only the container `movies` (with no path), the service stores the object directly in the container.

AWS Elemental MediaStore automatically deletes a folder when you delete the last object in that folder. The service also deletes any empty folders above that folder. For example, suppose that you have a folder named premium that doesn't contain any files but does contain one subfolder named `canada`. The `canada` subfolder contains one file named `mlaw.ts`. If you delete the file `mlaw.ts`, the service deletes both the `premium` and `canada` folders. This automatic deletion applies only to folders. The service does not delete empty containers.

Topics

- Rules for Folder Names
- Creating a Folder
- Deleting a Folder

Rules for Folder Names

Folder names must follow these rules:

- Must be unique only within its parent container or folder. For example, you can create a folder named `myfolder` in two different containers: `movies/myfolder` and `sports/myfolder`.
- Can have the same name as its parent container.
- Are case sensitive. For example, you can have a folder named `myFolder` and a folder named `myfolder` in the same container or folder because those names are unique.
- Can't be renamed after the folder has been created.
- Can contain uppercase letters, lowercase letters, numbers, periods (.), hyphens (-), and tildes (~).
- Must start with a number or letter.
- Must be from 3 to 63 characters long.
- Must not be formatted as an IP address (for example, 192.168.5.4).
- Must not contain underscores (_).
- Must not end with a hyphen.
- Can't contain two, adjacent periods.
- Can't contain dashes next to periods (e.g., my-.container.com and my.-container are invalid).

Creating a Folder

You can create folders when you upload objects. To upload an object to a folder, you specify the path to the folder. If the folder already exists, AWS Elemental MediaStore stores the object in the folder. If the folder doesn't exist, the service creates it, and then stores the object in the folder.

For more information, see Uploading an Object.

Deleting a Folder

You can delete folders only if the folder is empty; you can't delete folders that contain objects.

AWS Elemental MediaStore automatically deletes a folder when you delete the last object in that folder. The service also deletes any empty folders above that folder. For example, suppose that you have a folder named `premium` that doesn't contain any files but does contain one subfolder named `canada`. The `canada` subfolder contains one file named `mlaw.ts`. If you delete the file `mlaw.ts`, the service deletes both the `premium` and `canada` folders. This automatic deletion applies only to folders. The service does not delete empty containers.

For more information, see Deleting an Object.

Working with Objects in AWS Elemental MediaStore

AWS Elemental MediaStore assets are called *objects*. You can upload an object to a container or to a folder within the container.

In AWS Elemental MediaStore, you can upload, download, and delete objects:

- **Upload** – Add an object to a container or folder. This is not the same as creating an object. You must create your objects locally before you can upload them to AWS Elemental MediaStore.
- **Download** – Copy an object from AWS Elemental MediaStore to another location. This does not remove the object from AWS Elemental MediaStore.
- **Delete** – Remove an object from AWS Elemental MediaStore completely.

AWS Elemental MediaStore accepts all file types.

Topics

- Uploading an Object
- Viewing a List of Objects
- Viewing the Details of an Object
- Downloading an Object
- Deleting an Object

Uploading an Object

You can upload objects (up to 10 MB each) to a container or to a folder within a container. To upload an object to a folder, you specify the path to the folder. If the folder already exists, AWS Elemental MediaStore stores the object in the folder. If the folder doesn't exist, the service creates it, and then stores the object in the folder. For more information about folders, see Working with Folders in AWS Elemental MediaStore.

You can use the AWS Elemental MediaStore console or the AWS CLI to upload objects.

Note
Object file names can contain only letters, numbers, periods (.), underscores (_), tildes (~), and hyphens (-).

To upload an object (console)

1. Open the AWS Elemental MediaStore console at https://console.aws.amazon.com/mediastore/.

2. On the **Containers** page, choose the name of the container. The details panel for the container appears.

3. Choose **Upload object**.

4. For **Target path**, type a path for the folders. For example, premium/canada. If any of the folders in the path that you specify don't exist yet, the service creates them automatically.

5. In the **Object** section, choose **Browse**.

6. Navigate to the appropriate folder, and choose one object to upload.

7. Choose **Open**, and then choose **Upload**. **Note**
   If a file with the same name already exists in the selected folder, the service replaces the original file with the uploaded file.

To upload an object (AWS CLI)

- In the AWS CLI, use the **put-object** command.

  Example:

  ```
  1 aws mediastore-data --region us-west-2 put-object --endpoint=https://aaabbbcccdddee.data.
       mediastore.us-west-2.amazonaws.com --body=README.md --path=/test/document/README3.md
  ```

  Example return value:

  ```
  1 {
  2     "ContentSHA256": "74b5fdb517f423ed750ef214c44adfe2be36e37d861eafe9c842cbe1bf387a9d",
  3     "StorageClass": "TEMPORAL",
  4     "ETag": "af3e4731af032167a106015d1f2fe934e68b32ed1aa297a9e325f5c64979277b"
  5 }
  ```

Viewing a List of Objects

You can use the AWS Elemental MediaStore console to view items (objects and folders) stored in the top-most level of a container or in a folder. Items stored in a subfolder of the current container or folder will not be displayed. You can use the AWS CLI to view a list of objects and folders within a container, regardless of how many folders or subfolders are within the container.

To view a list of objects in a specific container (console)

1. Open the AWS Elemental MediaStore console at https://console.aws.amazon.com/mediastore/.

2. On the **Containers** page, choose the name of the container that has the folder that you want to view.

3. Choose the name of the folder from the list.

   A details page appears, showing all folders and objects that are stored in the folder.

To view a list of objects in a specific folder (console)

1. Open the AWS Elemental MediaStore console at https://console.aws.amazon.com/mediastore/.

2. On the **Containers** page, choose the name of the container that has the folder that you want to view.

   A details page appears, showing all folders and objects that are stored in the container.

To view a list of objects and folders in a specific container (AWS CLI)

- In the AWS CLI, use the **list-items** command.

  Example:

```
1  aws mediastore-data --region us-west-2 list-items --endpoint=https://aaabbbcccdddee.data.
     mediastore.us-west-2.amazonaws.com
```

  Example return value:

```
1  {
2      "Items": [
3          {
4              "Type": "FOLDER",
5              "Name": "ExampleLiveDemo"
6          },
7          {
8              "Type": "FOLDER",
9              "Name": "folder_1"
10         }
11     ]
12 }
```

To view a list of objects and folders in a specific folder (AWS CLI)

- In the AWS CLI, use the **list-items** command, with the specified folder name at the end of the request.

  Example:

```
1  aws mediastore-data --region us-west-2 list-items --endpoint=https://aaabbbcccdddee.data.
     mediastore.us-west-2.amazonaws.com --path=/folder_1
```

  Example return value:

```
1  {
2      "Items": [
3          {
```

```
 4          "Type": "OBJECT",
 5          "Name": "1512519711640.ts"
 6      },
 7      {
 8          "Type": "OBJECT",
 9          "Name": "test_file.pdf"
10      }
11    ]
12 }
```

Viewing the Details of an Object

After you upload an object, AWS Elemental MediaStore stores details such as the modification date, content length, ETag (entity tag), and content type.

To view the details of an object (console)

1. Open the AWS Elemental MediaStore console at https://console.aws.amazon.com/mediastore/.

2. On the **Containers** page, choose the name of container that has the object that you want to view.

3. If the object that you want to view is in a folder, continue choosing the folder names until you see the object.

4. Choose the name of the object.

   A details page appears, showing information about the object.

To view the details of an object (AWS CLI)

- In the AWS CLI, use the **describe-object** command.

  Example:

```
1 aws mediastore-data --region us-west-2 describe-object --endpoint=https://aaabbbcccdddee.
    data.mediastore.us-west-2.amazonaws.com --path=/test/document/README3.md
```

  Example return value:

```
1 {
2     "LastModified": "Mon, 20 Nov 2017 19:30:18 GMT"
3     "ContentLength": "2774",
4     "ETag": "2aa333bbcc8d8d22d777e999c88d4aa9eeeeee4dd89ff7f555555555555da6d3",
5     "ContentType": "binary/octet-stream",
6 }
```

Downloading an Object

You can use the console to download an object. You can use the AWS CLI to download an object or only part of an object.

To download an object (console)

1. Open the AWS Elemental MediaStore console at https://console.aws.amazon.com/mediastore/.

2. On the **Containers** page, choose the name of container that has the object that you want to download.

3. If the object that you want to download is in a folder, continue choosing the folder names until you see the object.

4. Choose the name of the object.

5. On the **Object** details page, choose **Download**.

To download an object (AWS CLI)

- In the AWS CLI, use the **get-object** command.

  Example:

```
1 aws mediastore-data --region us-west-2 get-object --endpoint=https://aaabbbcccdddee.data.
    mediastore.us-west-2.amazonaws.com --path=/test/document/README3.md README3.md
```

  Example return value:

```
1 {
2     "ContentType": "binary/octet-stream",
3     "ContentLength": "2774",
4     "CacheControl": "pre-commit",
5     "StatusCode": 200
6 }
```

To download part of an object (AWS CLI)

- In the AWS CLI, use the **get-object** command, and specify a range.

  Example:

```
1 aws mediastore-data --region us-west-2 get-object --endpoint=https://aaabbbcccdddee.data.
    mediastore.us-west-2.amazonaws.com --path=/test/document/README3.md --range="bytes
    =0-100" README4.md
```

  Example return value:

```
1 {
2     "ContentType": "binary/octet-stream",
3     "ContentRange": "bytes 0-100/2774",
4     "CacheControl": "pre-commit",
5     "ContentLength": "101",
6     "StatusCode": 206
7 }
```

Deleting an Object

You can delete objects using the console or the AWS CLI.

Note
When you delete the only object in a folder, AWS Elemental MediaStore automatically deletes the folder and any empty folders above that folder. For example, suppose that you have a folder named `premium` that doesn't contain any files but does contain one subfolder named `canada`. The `canada` subfolder contains one file named `mlaw.ts`. If you delete the file `mlaw.ts`, the service deletes both the `premium` and `canada` folders.

To delete an object (console)

1. Open the AWS Elemental MediaStore console at https://console.aws.amazon.com/mediastore/.

2. On the **Containers** page, choose the name of container that has the object that you want to delete.

3. If the object that you want to delete is in a folder, continue choosing the folder names until you see the object.

4. Choose the radio button to the left of the object name.

5. Choose **Delete**.

To delete an object (AWS CLI)

- In the AWS CLI, use the **delete-object** command.

  Example:

```
1 aws mediastore-data --region us-west-2 delete-object --endpoint=https://aaabbbcccdddee.data
    .mediastore.us-west-2.amazonaws.com --path=/test/document/README3.md
```

  This command has no return value.

AWS CLI Commands for AWS Elemental MediaStore

The following table shows the AWS CLI commands that you can use to create or modify containers and objects in AWS Elemental MediaStore.

Applies to...	Command	Description
containers (mediastore)	create-container	Creates a container.
containers (mediastore)	delete-container	Deletes a container. You can't delete a container that has objects; you can delete only empty containers.
containers (mediastore)	delete-container-policy	Removes a container policy from a container.
containers (mediastore)	get-container-policy	Retrieves the current policy of a container.
containers (mediastore)	list-containers	Lists all of your containers.
containers (mediastore)	put-container-policy	Replaces the current policy of a container with the specified policy.
objects (mediastore-data)	delete-object	Deletes an object that is stored in a container.
objects (mediastore-data)	describe-object	Retrieves information about an object that is stored in a container.
objects (mediastore-data)	get-object	Downloads an object from AWS Elemental MediaStore to a specified endpoint. You can provide a byte range to download only the part of the object that corresponds to the range.
objects (mediastore-data)	help	Displays information about the command being called. Append the keyword help to the end of any partial command line.
objects (mediastore-data)	list-items	Lists folders and objects stored in a container.
objects (mediastore-data)	put-object	Writes an object to AWS Elemental MediaStore.

Monitoring AWS Elemental MediaStore

Monitoring is an important part of maintaining the reliability, availability, and performance of AWS Elemental MediaStore and your other AWS solutions. AWS provides the following monitoring tools to watch AWS Elemental MediaStore, report when something is wrong, and take automatic actions when appropriate:

- AWS CloudTrail is a service that captures API calls made by or on behalf of AWS Elemental MediaStore in your AWS account and delivers the log files to an Amazon S3 bucket that you specify. CloudTrail captures API calls made from the AWS Elemental MediaStore console or from the AWS Elemental MediaStore API. Using the information collected by CloudTrail, you can determine what request was made to AWS Elemental MediaStore, the source IP address from which the request was made, who made the request, when it was made, and so on. To learn more about CloudTrail, including how to configure and enable it, see the AWS CloudTrail User Guide.
- Amazon CloudWatch Events delivers a near real-time stream of system events that describe changes in AWS resources, such as AWS Elemental MediaStore. Using simple rules that you can quickly set up, you can match events and route them to one or more target functions or streams. CloudWatch Events becomes aware of operational changes as they occur. CloudWatch Events responds to these operational changes and takes corrective action as necessary, by sending messages to respond to the environment, activating functions, making changes, and capturing state information. To learn more about CloudWatch Events, including how to configure and enable it, see the Amazon CloudWatch Events User Guide.

Topics

- Logging AWS Elemental MediaStore API Calls with AWS CloudTrail
- Automating AWS Elemental MediaStore with CloudWatch Events

Logging AWS Elemental MediaStore API Calls with AWS CloudTrail

AWS Elemental MediaStore is integrated with AWS CloudTrail, a service that provides a record of actions taken by a user, role, or an AWS service in AWS Elemental MediaStore. If you create a trail, you can enable continuous delivery of CloudTrail events to an Amazon S3 bucket, Amazon CloudWatch Logs, and Amazon CloudWatch Events. Using the information collected by CloudTrail, you can determine the request that was made to AWS Elemental MediaStore, the IP address from which the request was made, who made the request, when it was made, and additional details.

To learn more about CloudTrail, including how to configure and enable it, see the AWS CloudTrail User Guide.

Topics

- AWS Elemental MediaStore Information in CloudTrail
- Example: AWS Elemental MediaStore Log File Entries

AWS Elemental MediaStore Information in CloudTrail

AWS Elemental MediaStore supports logging the following actions as events in CloudTrail log files:

- CreateContainer
- DeleteContainer
- DeleteContainerPolicy
- DescribeContainer
- GetContainerPolicy
- ListContainers
- PutContainerPolicy

Every event or log entry contains information about who generated the request. The identity information helps you determine the following:

- Whether the request was made with root or IAM user credentials.
- Whether the request was made with temporary security credentials for a role or federated user.
- Whether the request was made by another AWS service.

For more information, see the CloudTrail userIdentity Element.

You can create a trail and store your log files in your Amazon S3 bucket for as long as you want, and define Amazon S3 lifecycle rules to archive or delete log files automatically. By default, your log files are encrypted with Amazon S3 server-side encryption (SSE).

To be notified of log file delivery, configure CloudTrail to publish Amazon SNS notifications when new log files are delivered. For more information, see Configuring Amazon SNS Notifications for CloudTrail.

You can also aggregate AWS Elemental MediaStore log files from multiple AWS regions and multiple AWS accounts into a single Amazon S3 bucket.

For more information, see Receiving CloudTrail Log Files from Multiple Regions and Receiving CloudTrail Log Files from Multiple Accounts.

Example: AWS Elemental MediaStore Log File Entries

A trail is a configuration that enables delivery of events as log files to an Amazon S3 bucket that you specify. CloudTrail log files contain one or more log entries. An event represents a single request from any source and includes information about the requested action, the date and time of the action, request parameters, and so on. CloudTrail log files are not an ordered stack trace of the public API calls, so they do not appear in any specific order.

The following example shows a CloudTrail log entry that demonstrates the CreateContainer action.

```
1  {
2      'awsRegion': 'us-west-2',
3      'eventID': '3b99ba80-fc04-44c5-8a2d-93e652088882',
4      'eventName': 'CreateContainer',
5      'eventSource': 'mediastore.amazonaws.com',
6      'eventTime': '2017-11-15T21:26:29Z',
7      'eventType': 'AwsApiCall',
8      'eventVersion': '1.05',
9      'recipientAccountId': '123456789012',
10     'requestID': '
           UNUR2YGS3HQRPM4LFJWUEOZLTSGK2KXX4KEMRFGVEP3WWXAOENJCI5VRWCWGHLKKQ33UVDQ4CSFAZAUL7G4FXPY
           ',
11     'requestParameters': {'containerName': 'MediaStoreContainer'},
12     'responseElements':
13         {
14         'container':
15             {
16                 'aRN': 'arn:aws:mediastore:us-west-2:123456789012:container/MediaStoreContainer
                       ',
17                 'creationTime': 'Nov 15, 2017 9:26:29PM',
18                 'name': 'MediaStoreContainer',
19                 'status': 'CREATING'
20             }
21         },
22     'sourceIPAddress': '205.251.233.176',
23     'userAgent': 'aws-cli/1.11.138 Python/2.7.10 Darwin/16.7.0 botocore/1.6.5',
24     'userIdentity':
25         {
26             'accessKeyId': 'EXAMPLE_KEY_ID',
27             'accountId': '123456789012',
28             'arn': 'arn:aws:iam::123456789012:user/Alice',
29             'principalId': 'EXAMPLE_PRINCIPAL_ID',
30             'type': 'IAMUser',
31             'userName': 'Alice'
32         }
33  }
```

Automating AWS Elemental MediaStore with CloudWatch Events

Amazon CloudWatch Events enables you to automate your AWS services and respond automatically to system events such as application availability issues or resource changes. Events from AWS services are delivered to CloudWatch Events in near real time. You can write simple rules to indicate which events are of interest to you, and what automated actions to take when an event matches a rule.

When a file is uploaded to a container or removed from a container, two events are fired in succession in the CloudWatch service:

1. AWS Elemental MediaStore Object State Change

2. AWS Elemental MediaStoreContainer State Change event

For information on subscribing to these events, see Amazon CloudWatch.

The actions that can be automatically triggered include the following:

- Invoking an AWS Lambda function
- Invoking Amazon EC2 Run Command
- Relaying the event to Amazon Kinesis Data Streams
- Activating an AWS Step Functions state machine
- Notifying an Amazon SNS topic or an AWS SMS queue

Some examples of using CloudWatch Events with AWS Elemental MediaStore include:

- Activating a Lambda function whenever a container is created.
- Notifying an Amazon SNS topic when an object is deleted.

For more information, see the Amazon CloudWatch Events User Guide.

Topics

- AWS Elemental MediaStore Object Upload State-change Event
- AWS Elemental MediaStore Container State-change Event

AWS Elemental MediaStore Object Upload State-change Event

This event is published when an object's state has changed (when the object has been uploaded or deleted). For information on subscribing to this event, see Amazon CloudWatch.

Object Updated

```
1  {
2    "version": "1",
3    "id": "6a7e8feb-b491-4cf7-a9f1-bf3703467718",
4    "detail-type": "MediaStore Object Upload State Change",
5    "source": "aws.mediastore",
6    "account": "111122223333",
7    "time": "2017-02-22T18:43:48Z",
8    "region": "us-east-1",
9    "resources": [
10     "arn:aws:mediastore:us-east-1:123456789012:MondayMornings/Episode1/Introduction.avi"
11   ],
12   "detail": {
13     "ContainerName": "Movies",
14     "Operation": "UPDATE",
15     "Path":"TVShow/Episode1/Pilot.avi",
16     "ObjectSize":123567890830,
17     "URL": "https://a832p1qeaznlp9.files.mediastore-us-west-2.com/Movies/MondayMornings/Episode1
           /Introduction.avi"
18   }
19 }
```

Object Removed

```
1  {
2    "version": "1",
3    "id": "6a7e8feb-b491-4cf7-a9f1-bf3703467718",
4    "detail-type": "MediaStore Object Upload State Change",
5    "source": "aws.mediastore",
6    "account": "111122223333",
7    "time": "2017-02-22T18:43:48Z",
8    "region": "us-east-1",
9    "resources": [
10     "arn:aws:mediastore:us-east-1:123456789012:Movies/MondayMornings/Episode1/Introduction.avi"
11   ],
12   "detail": {
13     "ContainerName": "Movies",
14     "Operation": "REMOVE",
15     "Path":"Movies/MondayMornings/Episode1/Introduction.avi",
16     "URL": "https://a832p1qeaznlp9.files.mediastore-us-west-2.com/Movies/MondayMornings/Episode1
           /Introduction.avi"
17   }
18 }
```

AWS Elemental MediaStore Container State-change Event

This event is published when a container's state has changed (when a container has been added or deleted). For information on subscribing to this event, see Amazon CloudWatch.

Container Created

```
1  {
2    "version": "1",
3    "id": "6a7e8feb-b491-4cf7-a9f1-bf3703467718",
4    "detail-type": "MediaStore Container State Change",
5    "source": "aws.mediastore",
6    "account": "111122223333",
7    "time": "2017-02-22T18:43:48Z",
8    "region": "us-east-1",
9    "resources": [
10     "arn:aws:mediastore:us-east-1:123456789012:container/Movies"
11   ],
12   "detail": {
13     "ContainerName": "Movies",
14     "Operation": "CREATE"
15     "Endpoint": "https://a832p1qeaznlp9.mediastore-us-west-2.amazonaws.com"
16   }
17 }
```

Container Removed

```
1  {
2    "version": "1",
3    "id": "6a7e8feb-b491-4cf7-a9f1-bf3703467718",
4    "detail-type": "MediaStore Container State Change",
5    "source": "aws.mediastore",
6    "account": "111122223333",
7    "time": "2017-02-22T18:43:48Z",
8    "region": "us-east-1",
9    "resources": [
10     "arn:aws:mediastore:us-east-1:123456789012:container/Movies"
11   ],
12   "detail": {
13     "ContainerName": "Movies",
14     "Operation": "REMOVE"
15   }
16 }
```

Working with Content Delivery Networks (CDNs)

You can use a content delivery network (CDN) such as Amazon CloudFront to serve the content that you store in AWS Elemental MediaStore. A CDN is a globally distributed set of servers that caches content such as videos. When a user requests your content, the CDN routes the request to the edge location that provides the lowest latency. If your content is already cached in that edge location, the CDN delivers it immediately. If your content is not currently in that edge location, the CDN retrieves it from your origin (such as your AWS Elemental MediaStore container) and distributes it to the user.

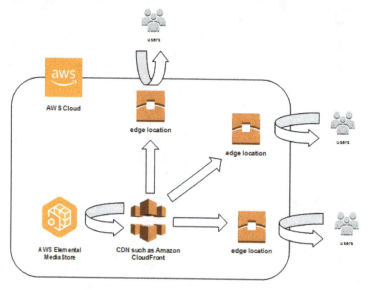

Topics

- Allowing Amazon CloudFront to Access Your AWS Elemental MediaStore Container

Allowing Amazon CloudFront to Access Your AWS Elemental MediaStore Container

You can use Amazon CloudFront to serve the content that you store in a container in AWS Elemental MediaStore. To get started, you attach a policy to your container that grants read access or greater to CloudFront.

To allow CloudFront to access your container (console)

1. Open the AWS Elemental MediaStore console at https://console.aws.amazon.com/mediastore/.

2. On the **Containers** page, choose the container name.

   The container details page appears.

3. In the **Container policy** section, attach a policy that grants read access or greater to Amazon CloudFront. **Note**
   The default container policy matches these requirements because it allows access to all AWS Elemental MediaStore operations, as long as the request is submitted through HTTPS.

4. In the **Container CORS policy** section, assign a policy that allows the appropriate access level. **Note**
   A CORS policy is necessary only if you want to provide access to a browser-based player.

5. Make note of the following details:

   - The data endpoint that is assigned to your container. You can find this information in the **Info** section of the **Containers** page. In CloudFront, the data endpoint is referred to as the *origin domain name*.
   - The folder structure in the container where the objects are stored. In CloudFront, this is referred to as the *origin path*. Note that this setting is optional. For more information about origin paths, see the Amazon CloudFront Developer Guide.

6. In CloudFront, create a distribution that is configured to serve content from AWS Elemental MediaStore. You will need the information that you collected in the preceding step.

Limits in AWS Elemental MediaStore

The following table describes limits in AWS Elemental MediaStore. For information about limits that can be changed, see AWS Service Limits.

Resource	Default Limit
Containers	100 (can request more)
Folders	Unlimited
Levels of Folders	10
Object Size	10 MB
Objects	Unlimited

Document History for User Guide

The following table describes the documentation for this release of AWS Elemental MediaStore.

- **API version:** November 27, 2017
- **Latest documentation update:** November 27, 2017

Change	Description	Date
New service and guide	This is the initial release of the video origination and storage service, AWS Elemental MediaStore, and the AWS Elemental MediaStore User Guide.	November 27, 2017

Note
The AWS Media Services are not designed or intended for use with applications or in situations requiring fail-safe performance, such as life safety operations, navigation or communication systems, air traffic control, or life support machines in which the unavailability, interruption or failure of the services could lead to death, personal injury, property damage or environmental damage.

AWS Glossary

For the latest AWS terminology, see the AWS Glossary in the *AWS General Reference.*